One Hundred Double Acrostics: A New Year's Gift

Myself

In the interest of creating a more extensive selection of rare historical book reprints, we have chosen to reproduce this title even though it may possibly have occasional imperfections such as missing and blurred pages, missing text, poor pictures, markings, dark backgrounds and other reproduction issues beyond our control. Because this work is culturally important, we have made it available as a part of our commitment to protecting, preserving and promoting the world's literature. Thank you for your understanding.

ONE HUNDRED
DOUBLE ACROSTICS.

A New Year's Gift.

EDITED BY
"MYSELF."

CRUSTY CRITIC—"Obscure quotations bagged from unfair literature!"—C. B. D.

HOPEFUL EDITOR—"Methinks a generous public will be lenient and indulgent."—H. W.

LONDON:
ROBERT HARDWICKE, 192, PICCADILLY.
1866.

DOUBLE ACROSTICS.

No. 1.

PRAY, all who buy this little Book,
Accept these wishes kind;
Be pleased its errors to o'erlook,
And to its faults be blind.

1. Glist'ning leaves of violet hue.
2. Silvery beams o'er waters blue.
3. My native Isle, fair freedom's seat.
4. This do, to make the two ends meet.
5. A Jewish maid, with locks of jet.
6. My dog's sad way, the naughty pet.
7. Come fill the goblet high with wine.
8. A merry lot in life be thine.
9. The clouds are gath'ring for a storm.
10. Pendent, it shines, in many a form.
11. My heart is rent with *grief* and woe.
12. He was my friend,—but now, my foe.
13. That noise again! those patt'ring feet.
14. O for my Cat to kill and eat!
15. Your humble servant, *this*, my last.

H. W.

No. 2.

My First implies perplexity;
A labyrinth my Second;
And both, without a clue or key,
Are tribulations reckoned.
Both mysteries, without the light
That helps to make Acrostics bright.

1. The Red Cross Knight with lance and brand
   Has fought the Paynim in Holy Land.
2. Swiss canton, Forest Canton called;
3. A Polish town, with a citadel;
4. Smallest of cantons, known so well,
   The Swiss will never be enthralled.
5. This is a populous village of Kent,
   Never, we hope, to be torn and rent;
6. Nor by fierce volcano's fires appalled.

A. A. W.

No. 3.

"Beneath our humble dwelling let us haste,
And here, unwearied, rural dainties taste."

"Cheerful at morn he wakes from soft repose,
Breathes the keen air, and carols as he goes."

1. Do not find fault, but eat it with its sauce.
2. I crave your pardon if I have given *this*.
3. A *diadem* of gems so rare;
4. She wore upon her golden *hair*.
5. From Afric's western shore
6. This animal we bore.
7. The last of his race, his name is heard no more.

H. W.

No. 4.

My First if real will priceless be
As the shine of the summer sun to thee;
Better than wine, and better than gold,
And also better for being old.

But war to the knife! if my Second comes,
Then sound the trumpets and beat the drums;
Yet if my First be false and fair,
It were better my Second himself were there.

1. "Chase him!" so a fairy spoke,
   "Light the torches round the oak!
   Pinch him, fairies, black and blue!
   Old, and full of mischief too!"
2. I am also old and rare,
   And my gems princesses wear.
3. Beggar or gipsy comes this way,
4. Upon my turf in June so gay.
5. This name is hated by the nations,
   Shuddering at his devastations.
6. Smoking our pipes, in peace we sit,
   Among our cushions, softly lit.

A. A. W.

No. 5.

Two Jewels, very bright and rare,
Worn by the beautiful and fair.

1. Stupid.
2. An article.
3. A point.
4. A victim.
5. A seaport.
6. Nothing.
7. Lifeless.

H. W.

No. 6.

Very dear to all are we;
Frequent source of misery.

1. Fluid.
2. Priest.
3. Story.
4. Water.
5. Measure.
6. Durity.

H. W.

No. 7.

Sometimes costly, sometimes clean,
Much more often dirty seen;
Though raised above the common clay,
Trodden underfoot to-day.

1. Livy will the tale unfold
   Of these cruel wars of old.
2. Tall and prickly grows the tree.
3. Here an Indian idol see.
4. Rank and beauty, lovely dresses,
   All these, now, one word expresses.
5. I adorn the neck of one,
   Supporter of the British Crown;
6. This is an adornment too,
   Arch that's light or dark of hue.
7. Liquid, burning, pure, and bright,
   Floating upon water, light
   As the swan's down or a feather;
8. Make at least the best endeavour.

A. A. W.

No. 8.

In holy bonds these two unite,
Each one will lose its name outright.
1. " O dark, dark, dark amid the blaze of noon!
   Irrevocably dark, total eclipse,
   Without all hope of day."
2. The state of him who o'er a convent rules.
3. A flourishing city of the United States.
4. One cup of this will clear the troubled brain,
5. When from my Fifth 'tis suffering racking pain.
6. How sweet his note as in his cage he sings!
7. O knowledge infinite!
8. Forget-me-not. H. W.

No. 9.

" Blest pair of Sirens, pledges of Heaven's joy,
   Sphere-born harmonious sisters!"
1. Among the Romans Five, twice told.
2. Many a tale in prose and rhyme
   Thus began upon a time;
3. Dark deceit did him enfold;
4. Ill-fated king! not always wise,
   We do not love his enemies!
5. Maternal ancestor, who gave of old
   Woes infinite to all of earthly mould. A. A. W.

No. 10.

Where the fair Priestess held her torch to light
  The trackless course of her adventurous lover;
That lover's native home—a city bright,
  Where eastern sunbeams kiss, and perfumes hover.

1. Dome and minaret and kiosk,
   Glitter about the stately mosque;
2. And glances the receding wave,
3. Breaking on islands where the brave
4. Sought to set foot, but found a grave;
5. Trumpets are heard the way they went,
   It may be for any instrument;
6. And clashing of weapons which deadly be,
   All of sharp steel as you may see.
   Take the weapons you like out of two or three.

A. A. W.

No. 11.

Oft made in haste,
Broken in paste.

1. A shoe.
2. An island.
3. A plant.
4. A melody.
5. A cheat.
6. A consonant and vowel.
7. A superfluity.
8. A throne.

H. W.

No. 12.

Pure and white,
Clear and bright.

1. 'Tis sweet.
2. A waterfall.
3. A river.
4. A metropolis.

H. W.

No. 13.

By me is spread
From Silvia's hand the showers
Most genial shed
Over the fairest of the summer flowers.

Green I grow,
And flourish in the heat of dim July;
Student who seeks to know
All wisdom, dwells on me with curious eye.

1. Flow of the channel as we cross its tide,
   Our breakfast ready on the other side.
2. I am of this opinion seriously,
   Behold! before us is a towering tree!
3. Part of a well-known motto here we see—
   Rest and be thankful! What will be will be!
   Say you it is not English, and not fair?
   A very common English name is there.
4. Sixth among five-and-twenty brothers tall,
   But Dr. Johnson says, a lizard small.

A. A. W.

No. 14.

In Heaven once was I ;
    We are in Heaven made ;
At least in poetry
    So it is said.
Combine us, we are useful too ;
You never should be without a few.

1. Call me early in the morning.
2. A milk-white lamb she leads.
3. It is fit and well adapted.
4. Somewhat learned he who reads
    Or writes this ancient measure.
5. How the roses grow we see,
6. And the ivy, too, encircling round
      The old and rugged tree ;
7. And all about the columns old,
      Where the Abbey used to be.

A. A. W.

No. 15.

"You raised these hallow'd walls, the desert smiled,
And Paradise was open'd in the wild."

"Around his form his long loose robe was thrown,
And wrapt a breast bestow'd on heaven alone."

1. "Laugh when I laugh, I seek no other fame;
   The cry is up and scribblers are my game."
2. Down in the dark deep forest glade,
   You'll find this flower beneath the shade.
3. On this and t'other side
   He doth disputes decide.
4. This wins the race at will;
   Insert it in your bill.
5. Hunting the hare.
6. Of many kings the name.

H. W.

No. 16.

At your door, and every day,
Sundays excepted, I come this way;
I wonder if people believe all I say?

At your door, and once a week,
Laugh and be merry, when I speak;
To do without us you vainly seek.

1. This is what the fairies do,
   By the moonlight on the dew.
2. Lady, shall we do the same?
3. Lady fair, is this your name?
4. Whimsical and deviating,
   Round and round the rings entwine;
5. Fabled care of toilette taking,
   Fairy, but not feminine.

A. A. W.

No. 17.

Without my Second, you will see,
   My First can never well be made;
On earth, and ocean, and the sky,
   That First may be at times displayed.
My Second may unite two nations,
Or signify our near relations;
Or, if this happens, it is plain,
The race must then be run again.

1. Of cheese, of cake, of butter, and of bread,
    With this King Arthur held his horse's head;
2. And I believe about King Arthur's time
    This people flourished in Italia's clime.
3. A little word expressing you and me;
    Sometimes our country or community.

A. A. W.

No. 18.

A scene of civil war, and the meaning of its name.

1. Upon the water sails the tiny bark;
2. Queen of fair features and misfortunes dark;
3. A weak old father;—pity's eye is dim;
4. This we should love, and help to float or swim.
5. Greatest of men, the children were of him.
6. We do not doubt she was both young and fair,
   The poet sang the "tangles of her hair;"
7. Maiden of very bright and fearless glances,
   Kate Coventry of Walter Scott's romances.
8. Friends and authors, wine and wood,
   When *this*, are best, I have understood:
9. The two last want *this* to make them good.
10. Our race, our erring nature, and our joys:
    Something divine it is, with sad alloys.

A. A. W.

No. 19.

Affirmative.
Negative.

1. Hiatus.
2. Volcano.
3. Emetic.

H. W.

No. 20.

"A man of loneliness and mystery,
Scarce seen to smile, and seldom heard to sigh.
But who that Chief? his name on every shore
Is famed and feared—they ask and know no more."

"The tender blue of that large loving eye
Grew frozen with its gaze on vacancy.
She looked and saw the heaving of the main,
The white sail set—she dared not look again,
But turned with sickening soul within the gate,
It is no dream! and I am desolate!"

1. "Then in one moment she put forth *enchantment*
   Of woven paces and of waving hands."

2.   "What is my *fault?*
   Where is the evidence that doth accuse me?"

3. "I'll not leave thee, thou lone one!
      To pine on the stem;
   Since the lovely are sleeping,
      Go sleep thou with them."

4. "I stood in Venice, on the Bridge of Sighs,
   A Palace and a Prison on each hand."

5. "Over the silken Ottoman
   Are thrown the fragrant beads
   O'er which her fairy fingers ran."

6. "She loved me for the perils I had passed,
   And I loved her that she did pity them:
   This is the only witchcraft I have used.
   Here comes the lady—let her witness it."

   A. A. W.

No. 21.

"Wake, dearest, wake! and again united,
  We'll rove by yonder sea;
For there our first vows of love were plighted,
  And there I'll part from thee."

1. "Merrily, merrily bounds the bark,
     Before the breeze she bounds;
   So shoots through the morning sky the lark,
     Or the deer before the hounds."

2. "Whom the Gods love die young."

3. "Tired Nature's sweet *sustainer*, balmy sleep!"

4. "I, sometime called the Maid of Astolat."

5.   "He flung
His epic of King Arthur in the fire;
He thought that nothing *fresh* was said,
             ——that a truth
Looks freshest in the fashion of the day."

6.   On the level green
He comes, the conqueror of king and queen.

7.   "Ere I
Could draw to part them was stout Tybalt slain,
And as he fell did Romeo turn and fly;
This is the truth, or let Benvolio die!"

8. "Weeks and months, and early and late,
To win his love I lay in wait!
Oh, *he* was fair to see!"

A. A. W.

No. 22.

"He shook the fragment of his blade,
And shouted, 'Victory!'
'Charge, Chester, charge! On, Stanley, on!'
Were the last words of Marmion."

"The tyrannous and bloody act is done;
The most arch deed of piteous massacre
That ever yet this land was guilty of."

1. Where sits the bee,
   Extracting liquid sweet.
2. This Duke, in merry days of yore,
   To wed an English Queen did soar.
3. "She silently a gentle *drop* let fall."
4. Take care of them.
5. "It is known
   "To be a lovely and a fearful thing."
6. Once, England's King.

H. W.

No. 23.

Earth will behold us never more;
Our glories may be yet in store;
Yet neither can exist, 'tis plain,
Without the other; 'tis in vain.

1. Foremost in fight was seen the blade
   In the hand of the Adrian renegade.
2. Hard is the answer, but it may,
   Perhaps, have been almost as hard to say.
3. A mimic war on a slippery ground,
   Where strategy better than strength is found.
4. Turn him out! this is a legal writ;
5. Though as he did this, a reward is fit.
6. False villain! let no soft eyes be dim!
   Dungeon and block should be ready for him.
7. See Tacitus; this was a people of Germany;
8. The miser is said to be this about money.
9. A sum that in general is punctually paid,
   Now, perhaps, called indemnification instead.

A. A. W.

No. 24.

Good wine will need me not, the proverb says;
A covert where its eggs the pheasant lays.
I help to clean your boots, I also grow
In this fair land, a source of wealth and show.

1. Diamond on the neck of beauty,
   Flaming gaslight doing duty.

2. A household officer about our Queen,
   To introduce, to bring in to be seen.

3. We slumber, free from danger and secure,
   For gold and title-deeds both strong and sure.

4. Build it upon a rock for a foundation,
   Here are the Lords and Commons of the nation.

A. A. W.

No. 25.

"'Twas noon; and every orange-bud
Hung languid o'er the crystal flood,
Faint as the lids of maiden eyes
Beneath a lover's burning sighs."

"I crown thee king of intimate delights,
Fire-side enjoyments, home-born happiness,
And all the comforts of the lowly roof,
Of undisturb'd retirement, and the hours
The long uninterrupted evening knows."

1. "One *woe* doth tread upon another's heel,
   So fast they follow."
2. Without these (my Second) no union could there be.
3. "The Queen of Night shines fair, with all her virgin stars about her."
4. "A wholesome herb that breath'd a grateful scent."
5. An apology.
6. Won by honours.

H. W.

No. 26.

"But yonder comes the powerful king of day,
Rejoicing in the East."

   A beam of light,
   How dazzling bright!

1. "The brave abroad fight for the wise at home."
2. A city in the United States.
3. "Even to the delicacy of their hands
There was resemblance such as *true blood* wears."

H. W.

No. 27.

"Here scattered oft, the loveliest of the year,
By hands unseen, are showers of violets found;
The redbreast loves to build and warble here,
And little footsteps lightly print the ground."

  "O speak, if voice thou hast!
Tell me what sacrifice can soothe your spirits,
Can still the unquiet sleepers of the tomb."

 1. A frightful chasm, this.
 2. A well-known name in history, mine,
  "A bold adventurer in my time."

3. By Florence, bright and gay,
I wend my silent way.
4. His moral character, excellent.
5. Wasteful.   H. W.

No. 28.

A Hero, and that for which he has been known to die.

"England! with all thy faults, I love thee still!"
"I like the Habeas Corpus (when we've got it)."

1. "Row, vassals, row! for the pride of the Highlands!
Stretch to your oars for the evergreen pine!"
2. "Albania's Chief, whose dread command
Is lawless law; for with a bloody hand
He sways a nation turbulent and bold."
3. "The Athenian's grave,
That *monument* which o'er the cliff
First greets the homeward veering skiff."
4. "Fosters, Fenwicks, and Musgraves, they rode and they ran!

They were chasing each other on Canobie
    Lea,
But the lost Bride of Netherby ne'er did they
    see!"

5. " On Linden, when the sun was low,
All bloodless lay the untrodden snow,
And dark as winter was the flow
    Of *the river* rolling rapidly."

6. " *Fie* upon Time, that for ever will leave
But enough of the past for the future to grieve!
Fie upon Time, that will leave no more
Of the things to come than the things before!"

7.   " No foreign foe could quell
Thy soul till from itself it fell,
And self-abasement paved the way
To villain bonds and despot sway."

A. A. W.

No. 29.

Pure as pearl, and white as snow,
Radiant colours too I show:
Crowned with jewels, wreathed in flowers,
Rosy Cupids count the hours;

And shepherdess, and courtly belle,
Combine to show my beauty well.
　We change the scene to other skies:
Country half barbarian,—vicious
People, flat-nosed and suspicious,
　Odd, but clever in our eyes.

Clear as crystal, pure as snow,
Yet I wear the ruby's glow;
In robe of azure I am seen,
Or vesture of Spring's early green;
Gold and fairy jewels grace
The fragile beauty of my face.
　" Drink to me only with thine eyes
　　And I will pledge with mine,
　But leave a kiss within the cup,
　　And I'll not look for wine."

1. The swords are drawn! heard, but unseen.
2. It is the entrance to the palace.
3. There came the noble Spanish queen.
4. The wine is dried up in the chalice,
　The oil burnt out; nought left to give,
5. To help the destitute to live.

A. A. W.

No. 30.

A Captive and its Prison.

1. Softening, healing, mitigating;
   To vegetable things relating.
2. Mental vision, an opinion,
   Picture in the mind's dominion.
3. Sign of poverty and sorrow.
4. This time last year, and to-morrow,
   Fruit we from the tropics borrow.

A. A. W.

No. 31.

These mean the same, as I suppose;
An interregnum both disclose.

1. Before light came this void was on the deep.
2. Odious, detestable, malignant too.
3. In port-wine good; and does it make one sleep?
4. On this we spend more than may be its due.
5. One thing is certain, whatsoe'er the sums,
   That this is always whence the money comes.

A. A. W.

No. 32.

My First perhaps has had its day,
But still you can go either way.
My Second's title ceased to be
When William the Fourth was King, you see.

1. Artificial fire.
2. A dusky gnome.
3. Lamentation.
4. A boatman.
5. Old England.
6. An alliance.
7. An old province.
8. The earth's shadow.

A. A. W.

No. 33.

One is long in the items, the other is round;
I dare say they cost much the same by the pound.
Nurse, tell me now, which of the two you would say
Will be best for the nursery dinner to-day?

    1. I call this being careless,
        And forgetful, and obtuse;
    2. And this a very pretty name,
        Though long for daily use.
    3. My good Sir, may I calculate
        On your vote for my return?
    4. But a long reverberation
        Was the answer, as I learn.

                      A. A. W.

No. 34.

"Weel mounted on his gray mare, Meg—
A better never lifted leg—
Tam skelpit on through mud and mire,
Despising wind and rain and fire!"

1. O'Shanter's brethren, not unknown to fame,
2. Joined with their bands the bold invader came.
3. General and Royalist, how good and brave,
4. I stand through storm and tempest, strong to save,
5. Where many a mariner lies cold beneath the wave.

A. A. W.

No. 35.

Twin sisters of sorrow are we;
The one you hear, the other see.

1. Sugar.
2. Water.
3. Holiday.
4. Fright.

H. W.

No. 36.

Antipodes.
1. Edge.
2. Tree.
3. Potash.
4. Bird.
5. Instrument.

H. W.

No. 37.

I have not tasted food to-day;
Fill up a bumper of Tokay.
1. Fire.
2. Whisky.
3. Law word.
4. An order.
5. Sorceress.
6. Forty shillings.

H. W.

No. 38.

"A wreath that is formed of flow'rets three,
Primrose, and myrtle, and rosemary;
A hopeful, a joyful, a sorrowful stave;
A launch, a voyage, a whelming wave;
The cradle, the bridal, and the grave."

1. "Morning is beaming o'er brake and bower;"
2. I fear this queen misused her power:
   Sad her story, and sad her fate,
   The Sea-God's pity came too late.
3. The sculptor's model, the painter's theme,
   Beautiful source of poet's dream:
4. This is the close of our life and its pride,
   Like the wave of ocean's receding tide.

A. A. W.

No. 39.

"At leaving even the most unpleasant people
And places, one keeps looking at the steeple."

"Loudly and merrily rang they then
Over forest and valley and sylvan glen,
And each voice was gay as a forester's horn,
And each heart was glad, for an heiress was born."

1. "And there were sudden partings, such as press
   The life from out young hearts, and choking sighs."

2. "Should England, dreaming of his sons,
   Hope more for these than some inheritance
   Of such a life, a heart, a mind as thine,
   Thou noble father of our kings to be!
   Beyond all titles and a household name,
   Hereafter through all times Albert the Good."

3. "Cassius, I am sick of many griefs."

4. "As plays the sun upon the glassy stream,
   Twinkling another counterfeited beam."

5. "A drop serene has quenched their orbs,
   Or dim suffusion veiled."

A. A. W.

No. 40.

Happy union.

" Say—pardon, king; let pity teach thee how :
The word is short, but not so short as sweet :
No word like pardon for kings' mouths so meet."

" My next, we are told, delights to dwell,
Strange mansion ! in the bottom of a well."

1. " It gives me wonder great as my content
   To see you here before me."
2. Who knocks ?   " Come in."
3. In Hungary you will find me famed for anti-
   mony.
4. Be satisfied,
5. Child.

H. W.

No. 41.

"Wide flush the fields, the softening air is balm,
Echo the mountains round, the forest smiles,
And every sense and every heart is joy."

"The pale descending year, yet pleasing still,
A gentler mood inspires; for now the leaf
Incessant rustles from the mournful grove."

1. "Roll on, thou deep and dark blue *ocean*, roll;
   Ten thousand fleets sweep over thee in vain."
2. French interjection this,
   Expressive, not of bliss.
3. "The fall of waters, and the song of birds,
   And hills that echo to the distant herds,
   Are luxuries excelling all the glare
   The world can boast, and her chief favourites share."
4. These little vowels three
   May ruin you or me.
5. If you desire to veil your face,
   Go to this town and buy your lace.
6. A deadly snare is this to all,
   To bipeds and quadrupeds small.

H. W.

No. 42.

Here the lavender is growing,
　　Purple to see;
In the honeysuckle's blossom
　　There lurks the bee.

1. He falters not, the chieftain brave,
　　Beneath the sable panoply;
"Wave, Munich, all thy banners wave!
　　And charge, with all thy chivalry!"

2. Come with me upon the river,
　　River flowing evermore;
Hark! beyond the rushes quiver,
　　Crowds of people on the shore.

3. Old man tottering and bending—
　　Under sorrows bending low;
Unto that we all are tending,
　　In this we are living now.

4. "Child amid the flowers at play!"
　　Chasing peacock butterflies;
Come, let us join the roundelay
　　Before the evening dies.

5. For this is the collector sent?
    Oh, must we sell the flock?
   " The bastion and the battlement"
    Are shattered by the shock.

6. Small name borne by a noble lord,
    See Horace Walpole's letters gay;
   Small ballad also doth record,
    " *The child* and her mother were walking one day."

7. Violets grow in the south of France.
    Come here, come here with me!
   " Sugar and spice," and a merry dance
    We'll have beneath the tree.

8. 'Tis a mighty emperor's name;
    Longfellow sings of a river;
   Oh, it brings reproach and blame
    In our history for ever!

9. To horse, to horse! and draw the sword,
    And bear this on your rapid way;
   Oh would my tongue could find the word
    To murmur what my heart would say!

A. A. W.

No. 43.

With a friend and these two things together,
We won't be bored in the winter weather.

1. The maps lie open, shall we burn the page?
2. Italian city must our minds engage.
3. To Indian province in the South we turn,
   And here most likely we have much to learn.
4. And being somewhat tired with this long flight,
   We'll end with an acrostic for to-night.

A. A. W.

No. 44.

Little Bag.
Great Brag.

United, contemptible.

1. Ginger beer.
2. Oliver Cromwell.
3. Pantheon.
4. A town of Saxony.
5. Finale.

H. W.

No. 45.

Insane.
Humane.
Dangerous when united.

   1. Great lady.
   2. Her name.
   3. Her cavalier.

H. W.

No. 46.

" I see thou art implacable; more deaf
To prayers than winds and seas; yet winds and seas
Are reconcil'd at length, and sea to shore :
Thy anger, unappeasable, still rages."

    " O mischief, thou art swift
To enter in the thoughts of desperate men."

   1. Sing low.
   2. No. 1.
   3. A termination.
   4. A mountain.
   5. Attractive.
   6. Tractable.

H. W.

No. 47.

"The sultry summer day is done,
The western hills have hid the sun;
But mountain peak and village spire
Retain reflection of his fire."

"And now the clouds in airy tumult fly,
The sun emerging, opes the azure sky;
A fresher green the smiling leaves display,
And, glittering as they tremble, cheer the day."

1.   "I know the gentleman
   To be of worth and worthy estimation."
2. In fair Italia's sunny clime
      This city you will find
   If so you wish, and you've the time,
      And on it set your mind.
3. "O hateful *blunder*, Melancholy's child,
   Why dost thou show to the apt thoughts of men
   The things that are not?"
4. "Love to her ear was but a name
   Combin'd with vanity and shame;
   Her hope, her joys, her fears were all
   Bounded within the cloister wall."

5. This river to mind you may not recall,
   It rises in Tibet and flows to Bengal.
6. Once near this ancient northern town
   Was fought a battle of great renown.
7. "O the dear pleasures of the velvet plain,
   The painted tablets dealt and dealt again."

H. W.

No. 48.

" How can ye bloom sae fresh and fair?
How can ye chant, ye little birds,
  Whilst I'm sae weary, fu' o' care?"

1. A shell.
2. A serpent.
3. The Bay of Biscay.
4. A robe.
5. Brompton and Kensington.

A. A. W.

No. 49.

"The night grows wond'rous dark; deep swelling gusts
And sultry stillness take the rule by turn;
Whilst o'er our heads the black and heavy clouds
Roll slowly on. This surely bodes a storm."

"From cloud to cloud the rending lightnings rage,
Till, in the furious elemental war
Dissolv'd, the whole precipitated mass
Unbroken floods and solid torrents pour."

1. "—— Till taught by pain,
   Men really know not what good water's worth."
2. "Where'er I roam, whatever realms to see,
   My heart, untravell'd, fondly turns to thee."
3. "She hears not of his death who bore him, and already for her son
   Her tears of bitterness are shed. When first
   He had put on the *livery* of *blood*,
   She wept him dead to her."
4. "In his brain,
   Which is as dry as the remainder biscuit
   After a voyage, he hath strange places cramm'd

With observation ; the which he vents
In mangled forms."
5. " Hark ! hark ! the sea-birds cry ;
In clouds they overspread the lurid sky,
And hover round the mountain, where before
Never a white wing wetted by the wave
Yet dared to soar,
Even when the waters waxed too fierce to brave ;
Soon it shall be their only shore,
And then no more ! "
6. " I drank ; I liked it not ; 'twas rage, 'twas noise,
An airy scene of transitory joys ;
In vain I trusted that the flowing bowl
Would banish sorrow and enlarge the soul.
To the late revel and protracted feast
Wild dreams succeeded, and disorder'd rest."
7. " Nature I'll court in her sequester'd haunts,
    By mountain, meadow, streamlet, grove, or cell ;
Where the poised lark his evening ditty chants,
    And health, and peace, and contemplation dwell."

H. W.

No. 50.

My nose.
My pet.

1. A basin.
2. Mysterious.
3. Stop.

      H. W.

No. 51.

A command.
The thing commanded.

1. Twins.
2. Back of the head.

      H. W.

No. 52.

Over bank and over brae,
Over heath and daisies gay;
Yes, I know she ran away,
And her name is Alice Grey.

1. The two were wishing for the self-same thing;
2. I took their messages, and some did bring;
3. Behave ourselves, you say, how then did we?
4. Why, civil in a very great degree.

A. A. W.

No. 53.

" Well, there is yet one day of life before me;
And, whatsoe'er betide, I will be happy."

" My heart is drown'd with grief,
My body round engirt with misery."

1.   " I'll have my bond,
And therefore speak no more."
2. " Hang there, my verse, in witness of my love."
3. " A Christmas box they bear."

H. W

No. 54.

Positive refusal.

1. A people.
2. Tooth-powder.

H. W.

No. 55.

" Man's rich restorative, his balmy bath,
That supplies, lubricates, and keeps in play
The various movements of the nice machine
Which asks such frequent periods of repair."

" And many monstrous forms we see,
That neither were, nor are, nor e'er can be."

1. A shallow sea is this, and yet a fish;
   Loud as a trumpet, gentle as a sigh;
   We hear it, see it, taste it on a dish;
   'Tis salt, and sweet, and harsh, and wet, and dry.
2. " The earth has nothing like a she epistle,
   And hardly heaven, because it never ends."

3. "How dear to me the hour when daylight dies,
　　And sunbeams melt along the silent sea!
　For then sweet dreams of other days arise,
　　And memory breathes her vesper sigh to thee."
4. A pantomime.
5. "Our country's welfare is our first concern,
　And who promotes that best—best proves his duty."

H. W.

No. 56.

Inquisitive.
Ditto.

1. Carriage without wheels.
2. Don't cheat.
3. Be cautious.

H. W

No. 57.

A visitor, and what he gives you.

1. The sea.
2. Do not exceed by half a grain.
3. Two or three.
4. Drops.
5. Assassin.
6. Fanciful.

H. W.

No. 58.

" With a friend and these two things together,
Happy we'll be in the summer weather."

1. "——Nature to advantage dressed,
   What oft was thought, but ne'er so well expressed."
2. Over the hills and far are we,
   Where the good Scotchman wished the Whigs to be.
3. A modern name that is advancing fast;
4. Perhaps it just as much deserves my last.

A. A. W.

No. 59.

Labour.
Patience.

1. A foreign capital.
2. A Spanish city.
3. A small Italian tribe.
4. It makes me dance.
5. A Persian province.
6. Twelve o'clock.
7. I'm just off.

H. W.

No. 60.

Dramatis personæ.

" The spirits I have raised abandon me;
The spells which I have studied baffle me;
The remedy I reck'd of tortured me;
I lean no more on superhuman aid,
It hath no power upon the past; and for
The future, till the past be gulf'd in darkness,
It is not of my search.—My mother earth!

And thou, fresh-breaking day, and you, ye mountains,
Why are ye beautiful ? I cannot love ye."

" Sovereign of Sovereigns ! we are thine,
And all that liveth more or less is ours,
And most things wholly so ; still to increase
Our power, increasing thine, demands our care,
And we are vigilant. Thy late commands
Have been fulfill'd to the utmost."

1. "The silver light, which, hallowing tree and tower,
   Sheds beauty and deep softness o'er the whole,
   Breathes also to the heart, and o'er it throws
   A loving languor which is not repose."

2. " The careful cold hath nipt my rugged rind,
      And in my face deep furrows eld hath plight ;
   My head besprent with hoary frost I find,
      And by mine eye the crow his claw doth
        wright ;
   Delight is laid abed, and pleasure past ;
   No sun now shines, clouds have all overcast."

3. " The humour rises, it is good ; humour me the
     angels."

4. "Gay sprightly land of mirth and social ease,
   Pleas'd with thyself, whom all the world can please."

5. "How rev'rend is the face of this tall pile,
   Whose ancient pillars rear their marble heads
   To bear aloft its arch'd and pond'rous roof,
   By its own weight made stedfast and immoveable,
   Looking tranquillity! it strikes an awe
   And terror to my aching sight! The tombs
   And monumental caves of death look cold,
   And shoot a chilliness to my trembling heart."

6. "I called not, my son." "Lie down again."

7. "Costly thy habit as thy purse can buy,
   But not expressed in fancy; rich, not gaudy;
   For the apparel oft proclaims the man."

   H. W.

No. 61.

Listen.
Look.

1. I die.
2. "Yes."
3. I breathe.
4. A pair.

H. W.

No. 62.

A pair of nutcrackers.

1. If you would a-fishing go
    (Cruel thing which I do hate),
   Turn this, shake it to and fro,
    If you mean to find the bait.

2. If you would be very wise,
    Study me with care and toil;
   Wear your brains and tire your eyes,
    Burning of the midnight oil.

3. He deserves a bitter word
    Who steals into another's throne,

  Like the ill-conditioned bird
   In a nest that's not her own.

4. Let us wise and merry be
  (Sage advice to keep in view);
 This, in the mean time, always see
  Between the old love and the new.

5. Hero of the sweetest tale
  That ever woke a maiden's sigh;
 The frost of years must much prevail,
  To read it, and our eyes be dry.

6. Cardinal, haughty minister
  Of the Bourbon days of old;
 Times cloudy, dark, and sinister,
  The coming woes foretold.

7. City of a Pagan splendour,
  O'er its ruins cluster vines;
 Scarce a column claims defender,
  Temple of the silver shrines.

8. So I end as I began:
  If you would a-fishing go,
 Take me with you, cruel man,
  Where the shady waters flow.   A. A. W.

No. 63.

" Birds, joyous birds of the wandering wing,
Whence is it ye come with the flowers of Spring?
We come from the banks of the green old Nile,
From the land where the roses of Sharon smile."

1. " Oh thou whose chariot rolled on fortune's wheel!
. . . . Thine eagles flew
O'er prostrate Asia; thou who with thy frown
Annihilated senates."

2. In many a fight, on many a shore,
In triumph he our banners bore;
His country gave him blessings due,
Victor of glorious Waterloo.

3. " Upon the wide, wide sea;
And why should I for others moan,
When none will sigh for me?"

4. Over the wall its blossoms hung,
Rich golden tresses thickly flung.

5. " In such a night
Did pretty Jessica, like a little shrew,
Slander her love, and he forgave it her."

6. "'Call the host, and bid him bring charger and palfrey,'
And then to Enid, 'Forward!'"
7. "*Receive* the coming, speed the parting guest."
8. "We were two daughters of one race,
She was the fairest in the face."

No. 64.

Gifted Orator.

"Thy words had such a melting flow,
 And spoke of truth so sweetly well;
They dropp'd like heaven's serenest snow,
 And all was brightness where they fell."

"I have seen
The dumb men throng to see him, and the blind
To hear him *speak*."

1. For this gay tournament I must prepare.
2. "None but the brave deserve the fair."

3. Single am I—a spinster, miss;
4. O what a bitter taste is this!
5. For this man's sins you need not weep.
6. Into your den I will not peep.
7. Look for this 'twixt eight and ten.
8. Faithless am I to fellow-men.

H. W.

No. 65.

I'm seen in a stocking; in hall and tower,
I guard the Queen; I mark each waning hour.

1. A cry.
2. A name.
3. A beginning.
4. A judge.
5. A Chinese province.

H. W.

No. 66.

Good news.
Happy finale.

1. "Good mother, do not marry me to yond' fool."
2. "You, ladies, you whose gentle hearts do fear
   The smallest monstrous mouse that creeps on floor,
   May now, perchance, both quake and tremble here."
3. "Go, sirrah, take them to the buttery,
   And give them friendly welcome every one;
   Let them want nothing that my house affords."
4. "Noble patricians, patrons of my right,
   Defend the justice of my cause with arms;
   And, countrymen, my loving followers,
   Plead my successive title with your swords."
5. "He that is giddy thinks the world turns round."
6. "Friendship is constant in all other things,
   Save in the office and affairs of love.

Therefore, all hearts in love use their own
    tongues;
  Let every '*this*' negotiate for itself,
  And trust no agent."
7. "What is thy name? and wherefore com'st
    thou hither,
  Before King Richard in his royal lists?
  Against whom comest thou? and what's thy
    quarrel?
  Speak like a true knight, so defend thee
    Heaven!"
8. "The appellant in all duty greets your highness,
  And craves to kiss your hand, and take his
    leave."

H. W.

No. 67.

"Oh! had we some bright little isle of our own,"
In a blue summer ocean far off and alone;
With nothing pretended, and everything true,
The roses all real and glowing of hue;

No darkened eyelashes, no dye in our hair,
No beautiful ringlets that never grew there ;
No pretty gold powder, no Madame Rachel,
Arabian perfumes, nor enamel as well !
Why, then all that glittered would really be gold,
And all pretty stories be true that we're told ;
And the two things to make this Acrostic so good
Never would have been thought of, as I've understood.

1. In Portugal a city this,
2. And this an Asiatic river
   Once signifying boundaries,
   Chinese and Muscovite to sever ;
3. This, left flank of Helvellyn is.
4. City that must be Chinese ever ;
5. Ambiguous now, so clear before ;
6. A Cardinal ; I'll say no more.

A. A. W.

No. 68.

"His eyes the hastening slumbers steep,
   And if ye marvel Charles forgot
   To thank his tale, '*he*' wonder'd not—
The King had been an hour asleep."

"*She* had the Asiatic eye,
  Dark as above us is the sky;
  But through it stole a tender light,
  Like the first moonrise of midnight."

1. "Now thro' the passing cloud she seems to stoop,
Now up the pure cerulean rides sublime.
Wide the pale deluge floats, and streaming mild,
O'er the sky'd mountain to the shadowy vale;
While rocks and floods reflect the quivering gleam,
The whole air whitens with a boundless tide
Of silver radiance, trembling round the world."

2. From India's coral strand
   This faithful woman came,
An orphan babe in either hand;
   Marica was her name.

3. "There will I make thee beds of roses,
   With a thousand fragrant posies:
   A cap of flowers, and a *girdle*
   Embroider'd all with leaves of myrtle."

4. "And will she love thee as well as I,
   Will she do for thee for what I have done;
   See all the pomps of the world pass by,
   And look only for thee, beloved one?"

5. "Now are our brows bound with victorious wreaths;
   Our bruised arms hung up for monuments;
   Our stern alarums chang'd to merry meetings,
   Our dreadful marches to delightful measures."

6. "My words fly up, my thoughts remain below;
   Words without thoughts never to heaven go."

7. "Ah! do not tear away thyself from me;
   For know, my love, as easy may'st thou fall
   A drop of water in the breaking gulf,
   And take unmingled thence that drop again,
   Without addition or diminishing,
   As tear from me thyself, and not me too."

H. W.

No. 69.

Naughty.
Boy.

1. "Of fare."
2. An initial.
3. It cuts itself.

H. W.

No. 70.

Exemplary.
Female.

1. Small pig.
2. The burden of proof.
3. Amphibious.
4. Her plaything.

H. W.

No. 71.

Puss.
Pony.

Bird when united.

1. Canvass.
2. "Love not" (in Latin).
3. Mirth.

H. W.

No. 72.

What would composition be
If attempted without me?
Far from honey'd. But without
Me, there is no sort of doubt,
Life would be unseasoned, flat;
Quite unprofitable, that.

1. This may be a sort of cherry;
2. Sparrow on chimney-top so merry;
3. Night of March, so blowing cold,
Brings my next, as we are told.

4. High we sailed in our balloon,
   This long word suggested soon.
5. At my last you must not frown,
   Turn the hourglass upside down.

A. A. W.

No. 73.

Angles four, and a line,
Which you will; the day is fine.
1. Division.
2. A measure.
3. And some confusion.
4. An alley.
5. A determination.
6. This disappears on one occasion.

A. A. W.

No. 74.

"The moon was watching on the hill,
The stream was stayed, and the maples still,
    To hear a lover's suit,
Which, half a vow and half a prayer,
Spoke less of hope than of despair;
And for its soft and sole reply
A murmur and a sweet low sigh,
    But not a spoken word;
And yet it made the waters start
    Into his eye that heard;
For it told of a most loving heart,
    In a voice like that of a bird."

1.   "From heavenly harmony
  The universal frame began;
    From harmony to harmony,
  Through all the compass of the notes it ran."

2. "What is love? 'tis not hereafter:
  Present mirth hath present laughter;
  What's to come is still *obscure*."

3. "Others for language all their care *devote*,
  And value books, as women men,—for dress."

4.   "On the Grampian hills
   My father feeds his flocks."
5.   "*This* from east to west
   Cheers the tar's labour, or the Turkman's rest."
6. "The west, that glimmers with some streaks of day,
   Now spurs the 'lated traveller apace
   To gain the timely *shelter*."
7. "By our country's woes and pains,
   By our sons in servile chains."
8.   "I make my way
   Where tumult, outcry, and alarms I heard."

A. A. W.

No. 75.

O! how oft, unseen, unknown,
   Does "the soul of feeling"
Muse on friends far off, or gone,
   Memory's stores unsealing.

O'er the track of years gone by,
   Pleased the spirit wanders;
Breathes o'er many a spot a sigh,
   Many a record ponders.

Scenes which long have disappeared,
  From their sleep awaken;
Sounds by loved lost friends endeared,
  Joys by them partaken.

Funeral tokens rise around,
  The full heart o'erpowering;
Urns with many a garland bound,
  Cypress-trees embowering.

Bright and fragrant then appear
  Flowers of recollection;
Bathed by many a holy tear,
  Nursed by fond affection.

O ye loved lamented few!
  Once to me united;
Heavenward, by each thought of you,
  Be my soul incited.

Has earthly love deceived thee?
Has earthly friendship grieved thee?
Has Death's strong hand bereaved thee,
  Of all most dear below?

A love which never changes,
A friend no time estranges,
A land Death's shaft ne'er ranges,
    It may be thine to know.

In vain have men asserted,
To cheat the weary-hearted,
That powers, by sin perverted,
    Themselves can calm the breast.

One hand, alone, unfailing,
Sin, grief's dark root, assailing,
O'er all within prevailing,
    Can give the weary rest.

  1. After the storm.
  2. Once Emperor of Rome.
  3. Expressly for my flute.
  4. In boudoir often seen.
  5. Hyacinth.
  6. Sweet-brier.
  7. A moiety.
  8. A plant.
  9. Not far off.
10. Sluggard.

11. Towards the end of a letter.
12. A decided negative.
13. Twice repeated.

H. W.

No. 76.

In the dickey,
On the box.
United, on the leg.

1. Patient.
2. The white boy.
3. A lake.
4. A county.

H. W.

No. 77.

My First as good as my Second.

1. Silence.
2. The third in five.
3. A type.
4. A lark.

H. W.

No. 78.

My First in my Second
Is pleasant to see,
When the snow's on the ground,
And the leaf off the tree.

1. Whence comes this imagination?
Whimsical, an aberration.

2. "He asked me, had I yet forgot
The mountains of my native land?
I sought to answer, but had not,
The words at my command."

3. Island of Ægean Sea,
Full of memories as can be.

4. Lastly, there may come before us
All the Muses in a chorus.

A. A. W.

No. 79.

One summer's eve, with toil and labour worn,
I fell asleep, and dream'd till early dawn;
This heroine fair appeared before my sight;
And this fantastic hero spoil'd my night.

"O! I am out of breath in this fond chase,
The more my prayer the lesser is my grace."

"But we are spirits of another sort;
I with the morning's love have oft made sport.
And, like a forester, the groves may tread
Even till the Eastern gate, all fiery red,
Opening on Neptune with fair blessed beams,
Turns into yellow gold his salt-green streams."

1. Alas! her fate—her grave—the deep deep sea;
2. O'er her the restless tide ceas'd not to *flow;*
3. *This* caus'd her death, O sad fatality!
4. Do not the same, or you may fall as low;
5. Had this her answer been when first they met,
6. We had not said my last on grave so wet.

H. W.

No. 80.

Ever moving, never still,
   Impatient is our pace,
And this our restless course until
   We've run our final race.

1. An opinion.
2. You can't spell this without me.
3. In the dairy.
4. Run away.　　　　　　　　　H. W.

No. 81.

Of greater value, single, here,
Than, when double, sitting there.

1. Upon my chin.
2. An acknowledgment.
3. A pair, and made of lace.
4. Paste.

　　　　　　　　　　　　　　H. W.

No. 82.

    Long may the noble towers there
    Survey domain and woodland fair.
    Long may the sound of hunter's horn
    Be on this valley's echoes borne.

1. "Merrily, merrily shall I live now,
    Under the *flower* that hangs on the bough."
2.   "From morn
   To noon he fell, from noon to dewy *night*,
   A summer's day."
3. "The winds were pillowed on the waves,
   The banners drooped along their staves."
4.   "Its deep blue eyes
  Kissed by the breath of heaven,
    And coloured by its skies."
5.   "Mollesson
  Thought us to *surpass*
  With a quaint invention."
6. "This world is all a fleeting show,
    For man's *deception* given.
  The smiles of joy, the tears of woe,
  Deceitful shine, deceitful flow;
    There's nothing true but heaven."

7. " He, pale as death, despoiled of his array,
   Into the Queen's apartment takes his way."
8. " The peacock in his laurel bower,
   The parrot in his gilded wires."
9. " You must know; but break, O break, my heart,
   Before I tell my fatal story out."
10.   " I've lived
    Amidst these woods, gleaning from thorns and *bushes*
    A wretched sustenance."
11. " The undiscovered country, from whose bourne
    No *wanderer* returns."
12. " This is an animal of Peru, whose wool is much used for clothing."
13. " What is friendship but a name,
    A charm that lulls to sleep;
    A shade that follows wealth or fame,
    And leaves the wretch to weep?"

A. A. W.

No. 83.

The fatal choice.

1. Shylock's bond;
2. Le Nozze di Figaro;
3. Bad company when melting;
4. A daisy chain.
5. What we should not do to any man.
6. A story-teller.

A. A. W.

No. 84.

My First and Second together weave,
And they will make a useful sieve.

1. Her Majesty.
2. Saved from the fire.
3. A proportion.
4. "In the eating."

H. W.

No. 85.

Adam and Eve.

1. A seat.
2. Celebrated tradesman.
3. A colour.
4. A favourite Psalm.
5. In all places.
6. Cooling.   H. W.

No. 86.

Suggestive.
Expressive.

Well cooked, a dainty dish.

1. Youth's resting-place.
2. Roman goddess.
3. Lampeto.
4. Whisper.
5. A duchy.
6. Unruffled.
                                H. W.

No. 87.

"Now sunk the sun; the closing hour of day
Came onward, mantled o'er with sober grey."

A cool retreat, my Second,
From summer heat is reckoned.

United.—Medicinal.

1. We can't have two.
2. A negro capital.
3. Avoid being married there.
4. Close fight this.
5. An obligation.

H. W.

No. 88.

"That chastity of look which seems to hang
A veil of purest light o'er all her beauties."

"Confusion thrill'd me then, and secret joy,
Fast throbbing, stole its pleasures from my heart;
And, mantling upward, turn'd my face to crimson."

1. "The multitude unaw'd is insolent;
   Once seized with fear, contemptible and vain."
2. "The dome's high arch reflects the mingled blaze,
   And forms a rainbow of alternate rays;
   And thus *I* shine, with many a changing hue,
   Like summer clouds beneath a sky of blue."
3. "But wherefore sleeps Sir Roderic——
   Apart from all his followers true?"
4. "Yet found I nought on earth to which I dare
   Resemble the image of their goodly light:
   Not to the sun, for they do shine by night;
   Nor to the moon, for they are changed never;
   Nor to the stars, for they have purer sight;
   Nor to the fire, for they consume not ever."
5. What grief is there!—"the heart is sorely charged!"
6. "Still on it creeps,
   Each little moment at another's heels,
   Till hours, days, years, and ages are made up
   Of such small parts as these, and men look back,
   Worn and bewildered, wond'ring how it is."

7. "' *These*,' following '*these*,' steal something every day;
At last they steal us from ourselves away."

H. W.

No. 89.

One.
Two.
Three.

1. Warranted.
2. Blue.
3. In Germany.
4. Caterpillar.
5. Over the door.
6. In at the window.

H. W.

No. 90.

1. Heavy blow.
2. Across the street.
3. Wake up.
4. In the ear.
5. On my box.
6. Mole.

H. W.

No. 91.

1. Not that.
2. An actress.
3. Vapour.
4. Quack.
5. Lengthwise.
6. A freak.

H. W.

No. 92.

One, two, three, four, five,
I caught a hare alive;
Six, seven, eight, nine, ten,
I let it go again.

1. Blockhead.
2. Samson.
3. I can't excel.
4. To escape from these,
5. O help me please.

H. W.

No. 93.

Two in the yard,
and
Two in the hedge.

1. Albatross.
2. Capers.
3. Box.
4. Paper.

H. W.

No. 94.

Beautiful Island of the West,
Ceres might in thy valleys rest.
Trust not the tiger in his den,
Nor treacherous wolf without his chain.

1. Revolutionist unquiet;
2. Short cessation of the riot;
3. Gloomy robes are round my Third,
4. Made of roses I have heard.
5. Romeo, Lancelot, Leander;
6. Little boat puts off the shore;
7. Ratcliffe, can you understand her?
   Miss Braddon, Edgeworth, many more.

A. A. W.

No. 95.

Black my First, or white, we see;
White my Second ought to be;
If gale or snow the day has vex'd,
My First should circle round my next.

1. From the shores of the Red Sea
    A resinous gum;
2. And a starry goddess
    The next may come;
3. Suggesting a zephyr,
    A flirt, or a swoon;
4. You will think of the deluge
    After it soon.

A. A. W.

No. 96.

"But I am constant as this northern *one*,
Of whose true, fixed, and resting quality
There is no fellow in the firmament."

"Her precious pearl in sorrow's cup
   Unmelted at the bottom lay,
To shine again when, all drunk up,
   The bitterness should pass away."

    1. Of the mind,
    2. And of the wind.
    3. Of the book,
    4. And of the cook.

H. W.

No. 97.

An excess in my First
Will ruin my Second.

1. A horse, or a bird, an apple, or fish;
Choose one out of these, whichever you wish.
2. A fish, or a precept, a cornet, or class;
In marble I'm made, in wood, and in brass.
3. A king, or a river, a powder, or tune,
A bank has contained me from July to June.
4. A portrait, a basket, a wanderer too;
For this was I made to beat black and blue.
5. I wound, I burn, I stiffen, follow, cry;
With finger, hand, and heart, and tongue, and eye.

H. W.

No. 98.

"Though lost to sight, to memory dear."

     There's not an hour
Of day or dreaming night but I am with thee;
There's not a wind but whispers of thy name,
And not a flower that sleeps beneath the moon
But in its hues or fragrance tells a tale
Of thee.

"When will ye think of me, my friends, when will
 ye think of me?
When the last red light, the farewell of day,
From the rock and the river is passing away,
When the air with a deepening hush is fraught,
And the heart grows burdened with tender thought,
    Then, then, let it be.

When will ye think of me, sweet friends, when will
 ye think of me?
When the rose of the rich midsummer time
Is filled with the hues of the glorious prime,
When ye gather its bloom, as in bright hours fleet,
From the walks where our footsteps no more may
 meet,
    Then, then, let it be.

When will ye think of me, my friends, when will ye
    think of me?
When the sudden tear o'erflows the eye,
At the sound of some well-known melody,
When you hear the voice of a mountain stream,
When you feel the charm of a poet's dream,
            Then, then, let it be.

Thus let my memory be with you, friends! thus
    ever think of me,
Kindly and gently, but as of one
For whom 'tis well to be fled and gone,
As of a bird from a chain unbound,
As of a wanderer whose home is found;
            Then, then, let it be."

 1. An olive-branch my First appears;
 2. Token of this,—to calm my fears.
 3. Here, 'neath the shade, I'll sit "*meanwhile*,"
 4. These tedious hours to beguile.
 5. I hear the leaves around me fall;
 6. The "*grave*" is near, last bed of all.
 7. Alas! alas! alas!

H. W.

No. 99.

"We part to meet again!"

1. The time is come that we must stand apart;
   My friends, to my Acrostics and to you
   I say good bye.   Another theme we start:
2. This one is prettier in Italian too,—
3. My Third a summer fragrance shall impart;
4. The banished one cares not if skies are blue.
5. Morn after night, and sunshine after rain,
   So clears the landscape to our sight again.
6. My friends, and a kind public, yet once more,
   But that our feelings conquer, being shy,
7. I might again propose to come before
   Your notice thus unostentatiously.
   I cannot promise quite to have in store
   Gilt and artistic borders for your eye;
8. But I am sorry now my work is past,
   And now my face must sadly look my last.

A. A. W.

No. 100.

"Farewell! but whenever you welcome the hour
That awakens the night-song of mirth in your bower,
O think then of him who once welcomed it too,
And forgot his own griefs to be happy with you."

1. My First is in powder,
2. My Second you see
   At a distance—of space,
      Or of time, it may be;
3. A principal street
      In a capital gay,
4. Where to-day and to-morrow
      Is flying away.
5. Pray do not be yielding
      To indolence now,
   Though a proper proportion
      Of rest I allow;
6. There is no occasion,
      For now we have passed
   To the ending Acrostic,
7.   And this is your last.   A. A. W.

IMPROMPTU.
MY LORD.
FALLEN.   H.W.

LONDON:
PRINTED BY WILLIAM CLOWES AND SONS, STAMFORD STREET,
AND CHARING CROSS.